WE SHALL NOT BE DENIED

A TIMELINE OF VOTING RIGHTS AND SUPPRESSION IN AMERICA

CAYLA BELLANGER DEGROAT
CICELY LEWIS

LERNER PUBLICATIONS ◆ MINNEAPOLIS

LETTER FROM CICELY LEWIS

CICELY LEWIS

Dear Future Voter,

You might be thinking, "Why do voting rights matter to me? I'm too young to vote." But every voice matters. Voting is necessary to a democratic society. The decisions voters make affect their lives and community, so it is important that everyone has an opportunity to vote.

Throughout the history of the US, many Americans from underrepresented groups have fought, suffered, or died for the right to vote. Their hard work and courage has allowed many to gain the right to vote. But challenges remain and affect many voters.

I created Read Woke Books to help you be an informed and caring citizen. I hope this book helps you learn more about voting and understand why the right to vote is important. As you read, think about the progress that has been made and how much further we have to go.

Yours in solidarity,

—Cicely Lewis

TABLE OF CONTENTS

TIME TO VOTE? MAYBE . . .

The 2020 United States election to choose the president neared. People asked how they would vote while also staying safe. The disease COVID-19 spread around the world. Being in small spaces with many people, as happens in voting lines, put people's health at risk.

What was the answer? Voting by mail.

Millions of people voted by mail even before COVID-19. It is a safe and needed way to vote for many people, such as people with disabilities or older adults.

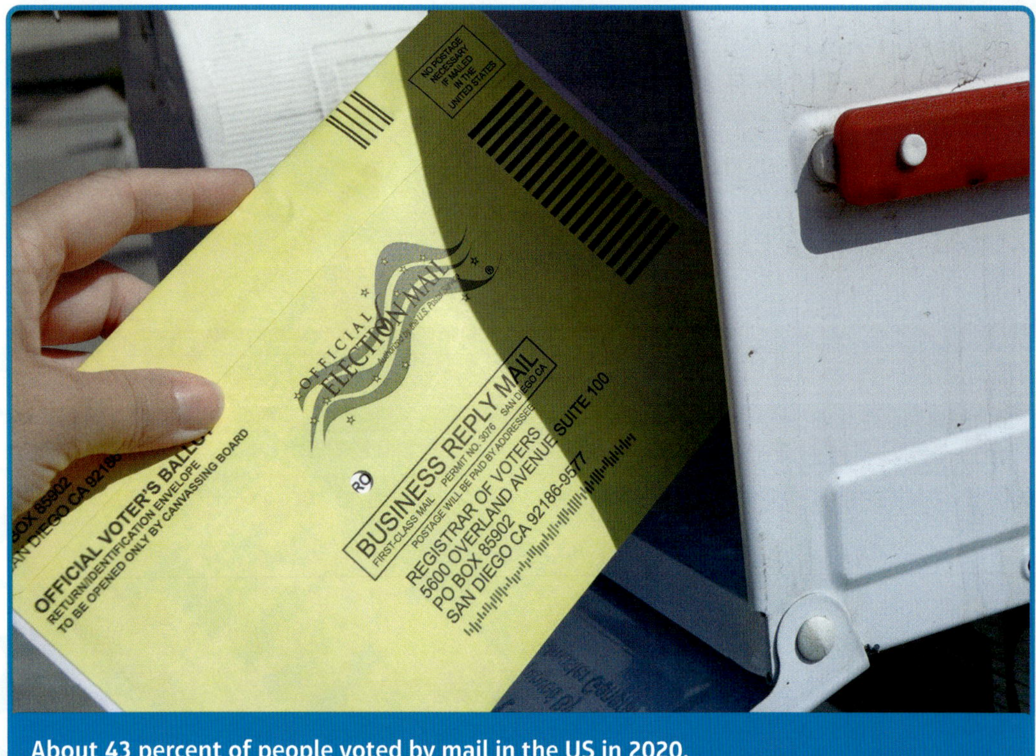

About 43 percent of people voted by mail in the US in 2020.

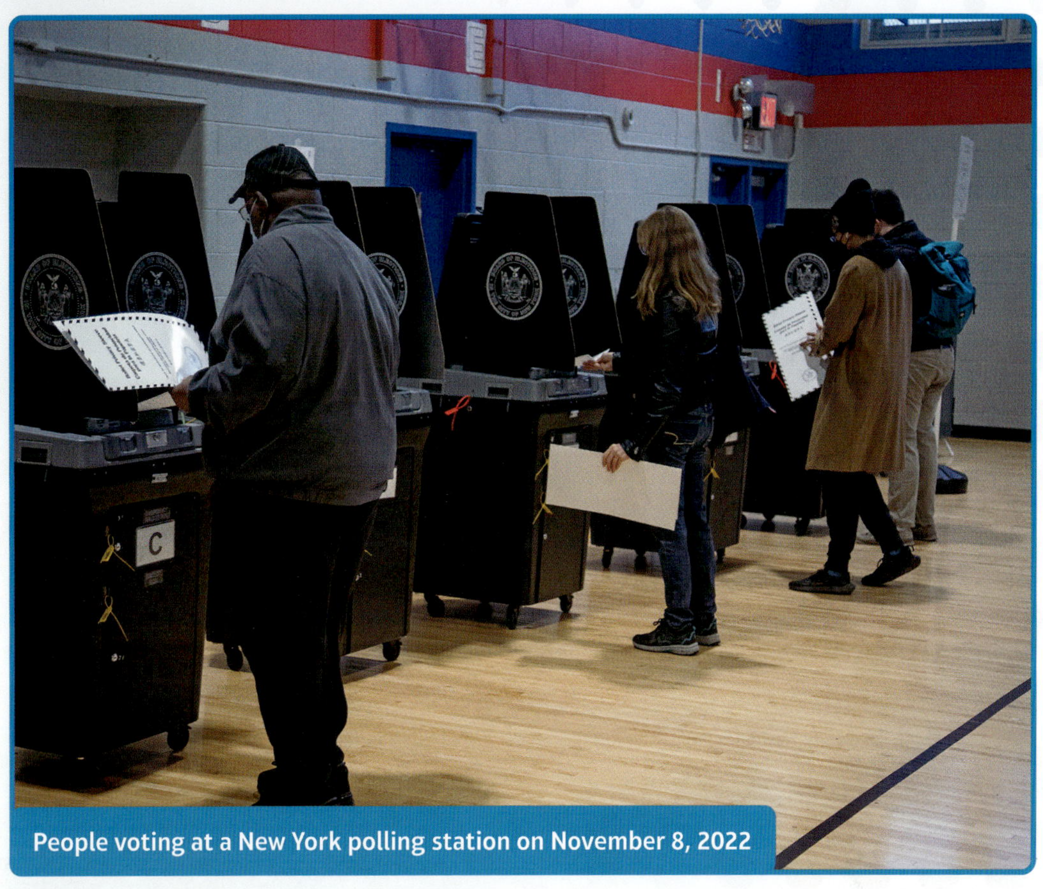

People voting at a New York polling station on November 8, 2022

Some people believe voting by mail leads to cheating in elections. So they pass laws to limit voting. More of these voting laws are passed each year. In the beginning of 2023, over half of the US states presented these kinds of laws. More than half of those laws limited voting by mail.

For over two hundred years, many people have fought for the right to vote. The fight continues.

CHAPTER 1

VOTING RIGHTS FOR ~~ALL~~ SOME

In 1787 a group of white men from twelve of the thirteen US states made the US Constitution. It listed the ways America would govern itself. It also gave states the power to control elections and make their own laws on who could vote.

An 1856 painting by Junius Brutus Stearns showing George Washington and other men at the signing of the US Constitution

The US Constitution

The men also passed the three-fifths compromise. It counted three-fifths of enslaved people in a state. A state's total population decided the number of votes that state would get.

Many states only gave the vote to white men who owned land. They limited voting rights based on a person's race, religion, gender, or wealth.

1787

The three-fifths compromise counts three-fifths of enslaved people in a state.

Most states only allow white men who own land to vote.

GIVE AND TAKE

The Naturalization Act of 1790 was the first law to say which immigrants could become US citizens. Free white immigrants who had been living in the US for two years could become citizens. Immigrants of color, servants or enslaved people, and most women could not.

People could not vote or own land if they weren't citizens. They also didn't have legal rights. But they still had to follow US laws.

An 1878 illustration showing immigrants arriving in New York City

1790

The Naturalization Act allows certain white immigrants to become citizens.

1807

New Jersey limits the vote to white men who pay taxes.

An illustration showing a group of men counting votes after an election

Some states made voting rights worse for certain groups. Before 1807 white women and free Black men could vote in New Jersey if they met the state voting rules. But after 1807, only white men who paid taxes could vote in the state.

In 1821 New York changed its state law about owning land. Black men had to own more land than they had needed to in the past to vote.

In 1828 Maryland passed a bill giving Jewish men the vote. Maryland was the last state to limit a person's voting right based on religion.

1821

New York makes Black men own more land to vote.

1828

Maryland becomes the last state to limit a person's right to vote based on religion.

CITIZENS WHO CAN *MAYBE* VOTE

Mexico and the US fought over the land that became Texas during the Mexican-American War (1846–1848). The war ended with the Treaty of Guadalupe Hidalgo. The treaty made an area of Mexican land part of the US.

The US made Mexican people living on that land US citizens. But they faced unfair treatment after becoming citizens.

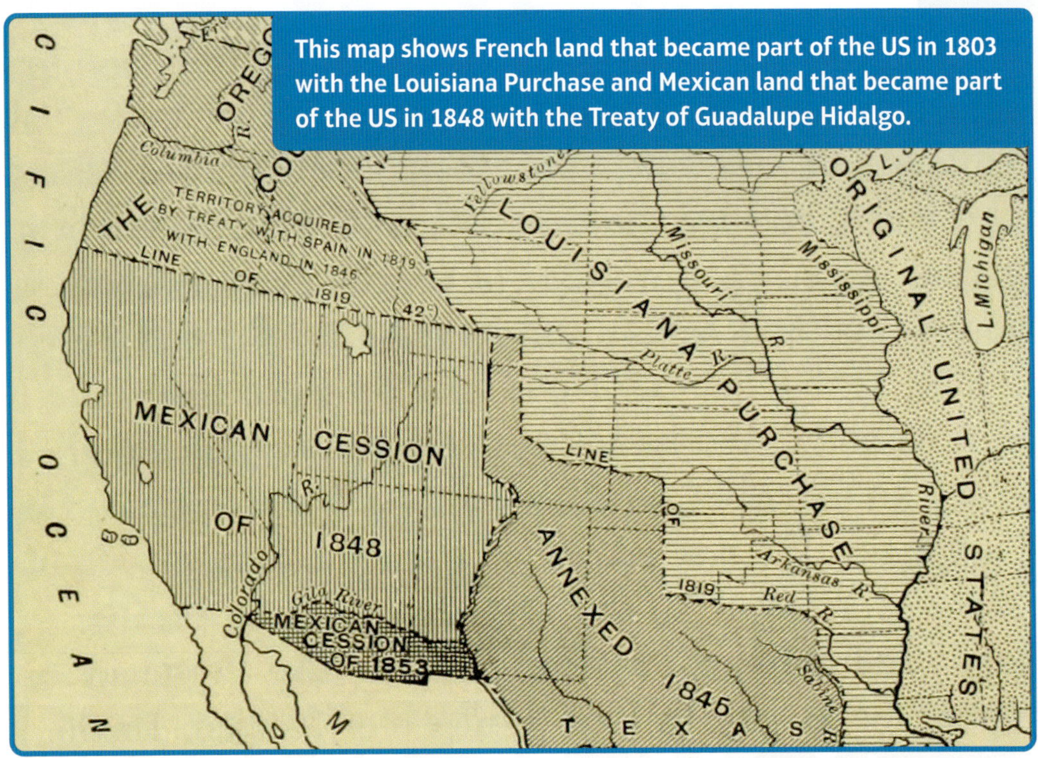

This map shows French land that became part of the US in 1803 with the Louisiana Purchase and Mexican land that became part of the US in 1848 with the Treaty of Guadalupe Hidalgo.

1848

Mexican people living on land that became part of the US become US citizens.

1856

North Carolina becomes the last state to limit a person's right to vote based on owning land.

NO NEED TO OWN LAND

In 1856 North Carolina became the last state to remove its voting rule on owning land. All white men in every state could vote.

Dred Scott

Dred Scott v. Sandford

WHO: Dred and Harriet Scott

WHAT: The Scotts were enslaved people that had lived in a free state. They sued for their freedom.

RESULT: The US Supreme Court ruled that enslaved and free Black people living in the US were not citizens.

1857

The Supreme Court rules on *Dred Scott v. Sandford* that enslaved and free Black people living in the US aren't citizens.

Wisconsin used absentee ballots in 1862 so soldiers could vote while away from home during the US Civil War (1861–1865). Each state had different voting rules. That meant military members in other states had no way to vote while away from home.

After the Civil War, there were two changes to the US Constitution. The changes gave more people voting rights.

THE US CIVIL WAR

The Civil War was largely fought over slavery. The Union wanted to ban slavery. The Confederacy wanted to keep slavery. Slavery ended in the US after the war. But racism and limited voting rights for Black people continued.

THE FOURTEENTH AMENDMENT

- **Passed in 1868**
- **Said all people born or naturalized in the US, including people who used to be enslaved, are citizens**

1862

Wisconsin gives soldiers absentee votes.

1868

The Fourteenth Amendment makes formerly enslaved people US citizens.

On December 10, 1869, Wyoming Territory became the first place in the US to pass a law giving women the right to vote. Women in the territory voted for the first time in 1870.

THE FIFTEENTH AMENDMENT

- **Passed in 1870**
- **Made it illegal to refuse someone the right to vote based on race**

When Wyoming became a state in 1890, it became the first state to allow women to vote.

1870

The Fifteenth Amendment makes it illegal to refuse a person the vote based on their race.

Women in Wyoming Territory vote for the first time.

CHAPTER 2

FIGHTING FOR CITIZENSHIP AND MORE

Thousands of Chinese men moved to the US for work in the 1800s. Some people thought that these men were taking jobs from white American citizens. So Congress passed the 1882 Chinese Exclusion Act.

The act blocked Chinese workers from entering the US for ten years. Chinese immigrants also couldn't become US citizens. They would not be able to vote.

Many Chinese immigrants came to the US for work such as mining or building the transcontinental railroad.

This is a 1910 poster showing the US Department of the Interior selling Native American lands. Think about who owns Native American lands and who has the right to sell them.

Reservations are areas of land a tribal nation holds and governs. The 1887 Dawes Act broke up these lands. The US government gave parts of the land to tribal members. White people took the rest of the land.

The act said that Native Americans who accepted the land from the government and worked the land for twenty-five years could become US citizens. They would get all the rights a citizen has and be able to vote. The act meant to assimilate Native Americans into white society.

1882

Chinese immigrants can't become US citizens because of the Chinese Exclusion Act.

1887

The Dawes Act allows certain Native Americans to become US citizens.

PASS THE TEST

Southern states passed Jim Crow laws after the Civil War. These laws made segregation legal.

In 1890 Mississippi began using literacy tests and poll taxes. The tests looked at how well a person reads or writes. The taxes were an amount voters had to pay. If people couldn't pass the tests or pay the taxes, they would not be able to vote.

In 1908 a public place in segregated Georgia allows only white people.

1890

Mississippi makes people pass literacy tests and pay poll taxes to vote.

VOTES FOR WOMEN

Colorado gave women the right to vote in 1893. White women in Colorado worked in the state government soon after.

Before slavery ended, it was against the law for enslaved Black people to learn to read and write. And they weren't paid for their work. This meant Black Americans struggled to pass these tests and pay poll taxes after slavery ended.

A 1943 sign in Texas reminding voters to pay their poll taxes

1893

Colorado women get the right to vote.

In 1898 Louisiana became the first state to pass a grandfather clause. It said that if a man, his father, or his grandfather had been able to vote before 1867, that man could also vote. It gave voting rights to poor white men who struggled to vote because they couldn't pass literacy tests or pay poll taxes.

The clause limited voting rights for Black people. Since many of their grandfathers were enslaved and not allowed to vote, Black men were then unable to vote. Other southern states passed their own grandfather clauses.

Beginning in 1901, voters in Alabama had to pass a moral turpitude test. Citizens who had been found guilty of crimes and didn't pass the test could not vote. But the idea of moral turpitude wasn't fully explained. Each county used the test in its own way. Many counties used the test to keep Black people from voting.

1898
Louisiana passes a grandfather clause.

1901
Alabama begins using a moral turpitude test for voters.

This 1901 map shows Montgomery County, Alabama. Each county in Alabama used the moral turpitude test differently.

RIGHTS FOR (WHITE) WOMEN

The National American Woman Suffrage Association (NAWSA) fought for years to get women's right to vote. But some chapters of the group didn't allow Black women to become members.

On March 3, 1913, NAWSA members marched in Washington, DC, for women's right to vote. Many women of color were in the march.

Seven years later, the Nineteenth Amendment passed. Women gained the right to vote. But many women of color still couldn't vote because of local and state rules.

SOME NATIVE AMERICAN CITIZENS

During World War I (1914–1918), over eleven thousand Native Americans served in the US military. For their service, Congress passed a law in 1919. The law let the Native Americans who served in the war become US citizens if they applied for it.

1913

NAWSA holds a march in Washington, DC, for women's right to vote.

1919

Native Americans who served in World War I can become US citizens.

THE NINETEENTH AMENDMENT

- Passed in 1920
- Made it illegal to refuse the right to vote based on a person's sex

Women march for their right to vote on March 3, 1913.

1920

The Nineteenth Amendment makes it illegal to refuse a person the vote based on their sex.

CHAPTER 3
EVEN MORE BARRIERS?

By 1924 Native Americans could become US citizens through marriage or by serving in the military. But many Native Americans weren't citizens.

President Calvin Coolidge (*front, center*) signed the Indian Citizenship Act on June 2, 1924. Here, he meets with members of the Rosebud Sioux Tribe at the White House in 1925.

Coolidge (*center*) meeting with Native Americans from the plateau region of the northwestern US in 1925

The US government wanted to assimilate Native Americans. They wanted to get rid of Native Americans' governments, cultures, and languages.

The government believed the next step was to make Native Americans citizens. They passed the Indian Citizenship Act in 1924. It made all Native Americans US citizens. But state and local laws kept Native Americans from voting.

1924

All Native Americans become US citizens through the Indian Citizenship Act.

CHANGE DURING WAR

The Soldier Voting Act of 1942 gave US military members a way to vote while away from home. The act tried to create a government system for absentee ballots. It didn't work because many states did not have the needed rules.

Four members of the Women Airforce Service Pilots during World War II

Seven members of the US Army Air Forces in 1943

US World War II soldiers filling out New York absentee ballots

The US and China became allies during World War II (1939–1945). To make relations between the countries better, the US passed the 1943 Magnuson Act. It ended the Chinese Exclusion Act. Chinese immigrants could apply to become US citizens and register to vote.

1942

The Soldier Voting Act gives military members absentee ballots.

1943

The Magnuson Act lets Chinese immigrants apply to become US citizens and vote.

Harrison v. Laveen

YEAR: 1948

WHO: Frank Harrison and Harry Austin, members of the Fort McDowell Yavapai Nation

WHAT: Harrison and Austin sued after not being allowed to vote in Arizona in 1947.

RESULT: The Arizona Supreme Court ruled in favor of Native American voting rights. But barriers kept many Native Americans from voting.

Seal of the Fort McDowell Yavapai Nation

1948

The Arizona Supreme Court rules on *Harrison v. Laveen* that Native Americans can vote.

1952

The Immigration and Nationality Act of 1952 helps more Asian Americans get the right to vote.

GAINS, SORT OF

The Immigration and Nationality Act of 1952 allowed more Asian immigrants to become US citizens. More Asian Americans were able to vote. But the US system kept favoring immigrants from Europe over Asia.

People of Japanese ancestry taking the Oath of Allegiance and becoming American citizens in 1953

THE TWENTY-THIRD AMENDMENT

- **Passed in 1961**
- **Gave people living in Washington, DC, the right to vote in elections for president**

1961

The Twenty-Third Amendment gives people living in Washington, DC, the right to vote in elections for president.

SELMA

On October 7, 1963, hundreds of Black people waited in line for hours. They wanted to register to vote in Selma, Alabama. The Black voters were not allowed to leave the line. Some people offered food and water to the voters. But Alabama state and local law enforcement responded to the Black voters and the people helping them with violence.

THE TWENTY-FOURTH AMENDMENT

- Passed in 1964
- Made it illegal to refuse someone the vote if they did not pay a tax

1963

State and local law enforcement use violence against Black people signing up to vote in Selma.

1964

The Twenty-Fourth Amendment makes it illegal to refuse a person the vote if they haven't paid a tax.

The Voting Rights Act of 1965 protected voting rights for people of color. It also forbid unfair treatment in voting laws.

After World War II, many people wanted to lower the voting age from twenty-one. People argued that since soldiers eighteen years or older could fight, they should be able to vote.

President Lyndon Johnson (*left*) signs the Voting Rights Act of 1965 on August 6.

1965

The Voting Rights Act protects voting rights for people of color.

During the Vietnam War (1954–1975), more people protested the age voting rule. Their protests led to the passing of the Twenty-Sixth Amendment.

THE TWENTY-SIXTH AMENDMENT

- **Passed in 1971**
- **Lowered the minimum voting age from twenty-one to eighteen**

Nineteen-year-old Karen Rogers voting in 1972

1971

The Twenty-Sixth Amendment lowers the voting age to eighteen.

A Florida sample ballot with multiple languages

The US has never had an official language. But people who don't speak English have faced voting barriers. In 1975 the Voting Rights Act expanded to include more languages on ballots. It also gave help at the polls for people who didn't speak English.

1975

Voting materials become available in more languages.

CHAPTER 4
RIGHTS GIVEN AND RIGHTS TAKEN

The Uniformed and Overseas Citizens Absentee Voting Act (UOCAVA) passed in 1986. It protects the vote of US military members and their families. It also protects the vote for other overseas citizens.

Absentee ballots and voting by mail are part of the act. Most states also have their own laws to allow these groups to vote.

Soldiers voting by mail at a US military base in Qatar in 2008

1986

UOCAVA protects the vote of US military members, their families, and other overseas citizens.

In 1992 the Voting Rights Act expanded again. It added more languages to ballots.

The National Voter Registration Act passed in 1993. It helps make it easier to register to vote. People can sign up at state motor vehicle offices and other offices or mail in forms.

People register to vote in California in 1996.

1992
The Voting Rights Act expands the number of languages used on ballots.

1993
The National Voter Registration Act makes it easier for people to sign up to vote.

Puerto Rico is a US territory. Puerto Ricans have been US citizens since 1917. But they can't vote in elections for president.

After suing for voting rights in 2000, a court ruled that people living in Puerto Rico can't vote in these elections. People living in other US territories also don't have this voting right.

TIME FOR CHANGE

In the 2000 election for president, some votes were counted wrongly because of old voting machines and processes. This led to the Help America Vote Act of 2002. It says voting machines have to be tested. States also have to follow government standards in elections.

MILITARY AND OVERSEAS VOTER EMPOWERMENT ACT

The 2009 MOVE Act expanded on UOCAVA's rules on mailing in ballots. It also formed a team to make sure states follow the act.

2000

A court decides people living in Puerto Rico can't vote in elections for president.

2002

The Help America Vote Act prevents votes from being wrongly counted.

Elections supervisors reviewing overseas absentee ballots in 2000

2009

The MOVE Act strengthens rules on mail-in ballots.

Shelby County v. Holder

YEAR: 2013

WHO: Shelby County, Alabama

WHAT: Shelby County said that Section 5 of the Voting Rights Act is unconstitutional. Section 5 made certain states get government approval before changing their voting laws.

RESULT: The Supreme Court ruled that Section 4(b) of the act is unconstitutional. Section 4(b) said which states were part of Section 5. Without Section 4(b), no states would need the approval from Section 5.

On February 27, 2013, activists hold voting rights signs outside the US Supreme Court ahead of *Shelby County v. Holder*.

2013

The Supreme Court rules on *Shelby County v. Holder* that it is unconstitutional to say which states need government approval before changing voting laws.

Alabama has been using the moral turpitude test since 1901. In 2017 Alabama passed HB282. The bill listed moral turpitude crimes for the first time. More people charged with crimes were able to vote.

Some states have laws that stop people who have been charged with crimes from voting if they owe fees to the state. These fees can be costly. People who can't pay the fees can't vote.

A voter going to a polling station in Birmingham, Alabama, in 2017

2017

An Alabama bill lists moral turpitude crimes that disqualify a person from voting.

In 2019 judges in North Carolina made the state government redraw their voting district maps. Voting districts are areas where groups of voters will be represented by an elected official.

The judges found that the state had been gerrymandering. That is when voting districts are changed to favor one political party. This can affect election results and how votes from different racial groups are counted.

North Carolina state representative John Szoka reviewing a redistricting map during a 2019 meeting

2019

North Carolina redraws their voting district maps.

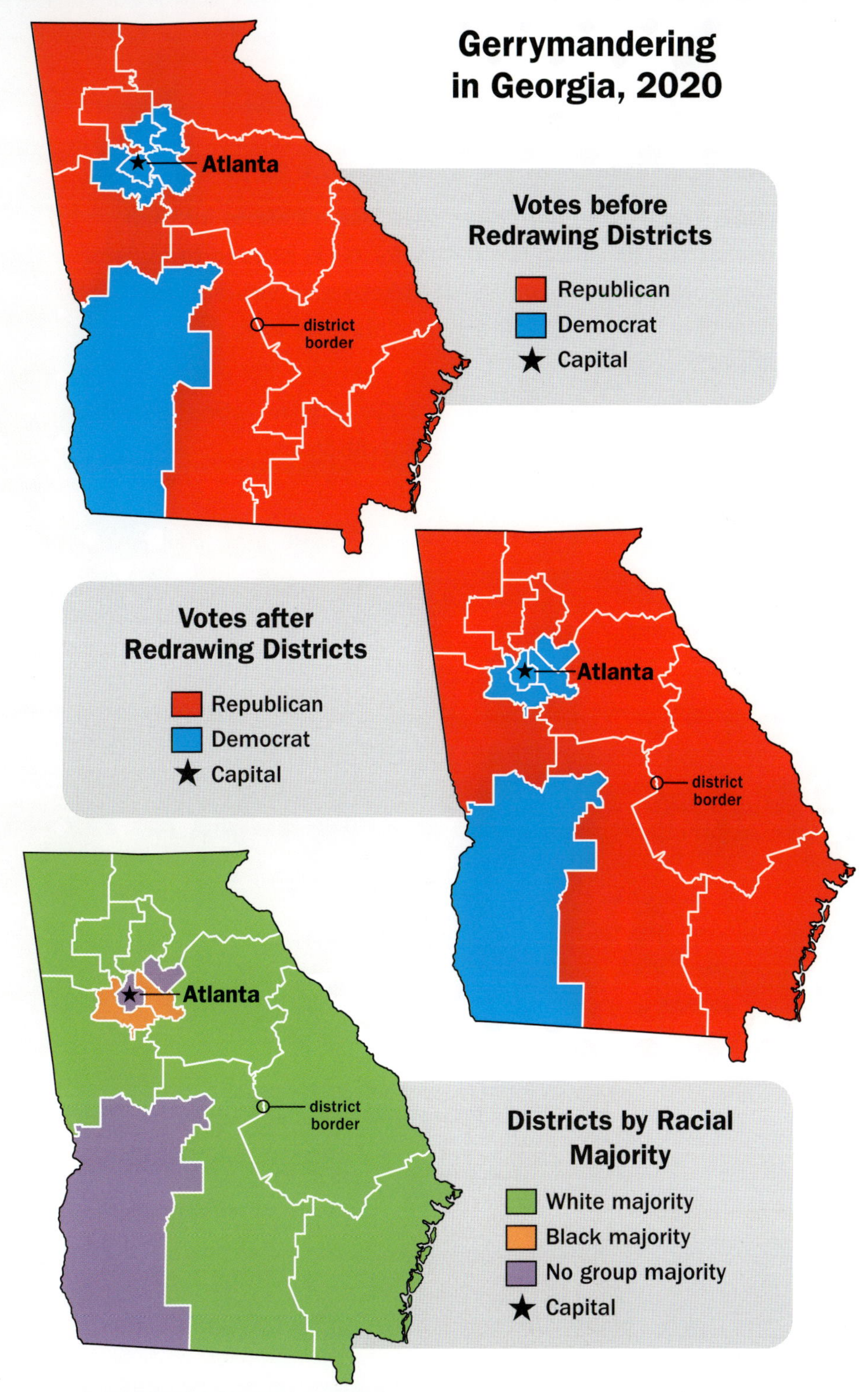
Gerrymandering in Georgia, 2020
Atlanta
district border
Votes before Redrawing Districts
Republican
Democrat
Capital
Votes after Redrawing Districts
Republican
Democrat
Capital
Atlanta
district border
Atlanta
district border
Districts by Racial Majority
White majority
Black majority
No group majority
Capital

Brakebill v. Jaeger

WHO: Spirit Lake Tribe and Standing Rock Sioux Tribe

WHAT: The two tribal nations sued North Dakota for their housing and ID voting laws. An address is needed to register to vote. Many homes on North Dakota reservations don't have addresses. Native Americans may also not have an ID with an address.

RESULT: The lawsuit settled in 2020. It gave voting protection to Native Americans living on reservations.

Rock the Native Vote coordinator Codie Horse-Topetchy opens a stall at the Comanche Nation in 2023 to encourage Native Americans to vote.

2020

Brakebill v. Jaeger **ensures that Native Americans living on reservations have voting protections.**

FUTURE VOTERS

A lot of progress has been made to give people voting rights. But more work can be done.

Voting is how our country chooses government leaders to make important decisions that affect all our lives. When one citizen is denied their right to vote, their voice is silenced. Everyone deserves a voice.

Even if you are not old enough to vote, you can make a difference. Get informed about our country's leaders. Make your voice heard. And spread the word about the importance of voting!

People voting in North Carolina in 2022

2023

Over half of the US states present laws to limit voting.

JULIANA V. UNITED STATES

In 2015 twenty-one young Americans, all under the minimum voting age, filed the lawsuit *Juliana v. United States*. They sued the US government about climate change. They argued that by taking action that causes climate change, the government failed to uphold their constitutional rights. As of July 2023, the lawsuit was on its way to trial.

This is just one example of young Americans working for change. You have the power to impact voting and laws that are made, even without being able to vote. Consider the issues you care about, and look at the Take Action page for ways to get started.

The young people that filed the lawsuit *Juliana v. United States* attend a hearing on June 4, 2019.

TAKE ACTION

Think about the ways your state and local government affect you. Even though you may be too young to vote, your voice can be heard! Here are some ideas:

- ✔ Talk to your teachers about holding a mock election in your school.
- ✔ Volunteer with a trusted adult to help register people to vote.
- ✔ Watch a political debate with your family and discuss it.
- ✔ Research an issue and share the information with others, such as by creating a poster.
- ✔ Find out who is running in elections near you, and learn about what they stand for.

REFLECT

- ✔ You must be eighteen years old or older to vote in the US. Why do you think the voting age should or should not be lowered?
- ✔ Consider the literacy tests, poll taxes, and other actions used to prevent certain groups of people from voting. How is this harmful? How does knowing the history of these actions help shape the future of voting?
- ✔ Think about why it has taken so long for many people to get the right to vote and why some people still aren't allowed to vote. Who is being left out? Why does this matter?
- ✔ Laws that limit voting rights are still being made each year. Consider who is making these laws. What is their motive?
- ✔ Is voting a right or a privilege? What is the difference between the two? Do you think some people shouldn't be allowed to vote? Why or why not?

GLOSSARY

absentee ballot: a vote cast by someone who cannot get to a polling place

amendment: a change in a law or document

assimilate: to absorb into the culture of a population or group

citizenship: being a legal member of a country

disability: a physical or mental condition that makes it harder to do certain activities

immigrant: a person who moves to and lives in a country other than their native country

moral turpitude: an action or behavior that does not follow a community's standards of behavior

naturalization: becoming a citizen of a country other than the country a person was born in

registration: to register, or sign up, to vote

represent: standing for someone or serving as a sign of something

segregation: a legal system of forced separation, done specifically by race. In the US, segregation was enforced by the people in power, which historically have been white men.

READ WOKE READING LIST

Bellanger DeGroat, Cayla. *Native Voting Rights and Sovereignty: Recognizing Indigenous Voices in Government*. Minneapolis: Lerner Publications, 2025.

Britannica Kids: Voting Rights Act
https://kids.britannica.com/students/article/Voting-Rights-Act/631613

Library of Congress: The Right to Vote
https://www.loc.gov/classroom-materials/elections/right-to-vote/

National Geographic Kids: Battles for the Ballot
https://kids.nationalgeographic.com/history/article/we-want-to-vote-battles-for-the-ballot

PBS LearningMedia: The History of Voting Rights
https://tpt.pbslearningmedia.org/resource/ush22-soc-votinghistory/the-history-of-voting-rights-interactive-timeline/

Smith, Erin Geiger. *Thank You for Voting Young Readers' Edition: The Past, Present, and Future of Voting*. New York: Quill Tree Books, 2021.

Tyner, Dr. Artika R. *Black Voter Suppression: The Fight for the Right to Vote*. Minneapolis: Lerner Publications, 2021.

Winn, Kevin P., and Kelisa Wing. *Voting Rights*. Ann Arbor, MI: Cherry Lake, 2021.

INDEX

PHOTO ACKNOWLEDGMENTS

Image credits: Simone Hogan/Alamy, p. 4; Michael Nagle/Xinhua/Getty Images, p. 5; Ian Dagnall/Alamy, p. 6; Joseph Sohm/Getty Images, p. 7; Bettmann Archive/Getty Images, pp. 8, 11, 30; Library of Congress/Interim Archives/Getty Images, p. 9; Alamy, p. 10; Science History Images/Alamy, pp. 13, 23, 29; CPA Media Pte Ltd/Alamy, p. 14; B Christopher/Alamy, p. 15; Heritage Art/Heritage Images/Getty Images, p. 16; Russell Lee/PhotoQuest/Getty Images, p. 17; Wikimedia Commons PD, p. 19; Library of Congress, p. 21; Everett Collection Inc/Alamy, p. 22; US Air Force, p. 24 (top); Archive Photos/Getty Images, p. 24 (bottom); Corbis/Getty Images, p. 25; Marine 69-71/Wikimedia Commons (CC BY-SA 4.0 DEED), p. 26; © Bridgeman Images, p. 27; Jeffrey Isaac Greenberg 9+/Alamy, p. 31; Official Army Photo/Dustin Senger/Alamy, p. 32; David Butow/Corbis/Getty Images, p. 33; Alex Wong/Newsmakers/Getty Images, p. 35; MANDEL NGAN/AFP/Getty Images, p. 36; Bill Clark/CQ Roll Call/Getty Images, p. 37; AP Photo/Robert Willett/The News & Observer, p. 38; CHANDAN KHANNA/AFP/Getty Images, p. 40; Peter Zay/Anadolu Agency/Getty Images, p. 41; AP Photo/Robin Loznak, p. 42. Cicely Lewis portrait photo by Fernando Decillis. Design elements: pashabo/Shutterstock; Marina Santiaga/Shutterstock; Alexander Yurkevich/Shutterstock; aomvector/Shutterstock.

Cover: Marina Santiaga/Shutterstock; Alexander Yurkevich/Shutterstock; aomvector/Shutterstock.

To future voters everywhere. Get ready to make your mark.

—Cicely Lewis

To Jory and Ezra, future voters

—Cayla Bellanger DeGroat

Content consultant: Dr. Cleopatra Warren, Atlanta Public Schools, Atlanta, Georgia

Lerner Publications Company
An imprint of Lerner Publishing Group, Inc.
241 First Avenue North
Minneapolis, MN 55401 USA

For reading levels and more information, look up this title at www.lernerbooks.com.

Main body text set in Aptifer Sans LT Pro.
Typeface provided by Linotype AG.

Maps on p. 39 by Laura K. Westlund

Editor: Brianna Kaiser **Designer:** Kim Morales **Photo Editor:** Giliane Mansfeldt
Lerner team: Martha Kranes, Sue Marquis

Library of Congress Cataloging-in-Publication Data

Names: Lewis, Cicely, author. | DeGroat, Cayla Bellanger, author.
Title: We shall not be denied : a timeline of voting rights and suppression in America / Cicely Lewis, Cayla Bellanger DeGroat.
Description: Minneapolis : Lerner Publications, 2025. | Includes bibliographical references and index. | Audience: Ages 9–14 | Audience: Grades 4–6 | Summary: "This title takes an in-depth look at voting rights in the US, particularly examining when certain groups of people won the right to vote. Special features expand on the text and highlight why voting is important"— Provided by publisher.
Identifiers: LCCN 2023031891 (print) | LCCN 2023031892 (ebook) | ISBN 9798765611586 (library binding) | ISBN 9798765629185 (paperback) | ISBN 9798765636046 (epub)
Subjects: LCSH: Suffrage—United States—Juvenile literature.
Classification: LCC JK1846 .L49 2024 (print) | LCC JK1846 (ebook) | DDC 324.6/20973—dc23/eng/20231226

LC record available at https://lccn.loc.gov/2023031891
LC ebook record available at https://lccn.loc.gov/2023031892

Manufactured in the United States of America
2-1011727-51780-10/16/2024